PEOPLE WHO CHANGED AMERICA

THE
PROGRESSIVES

MONICA HALPERN

Produced through the worldwide resources of the National Geographic Society, John M. Fahey, Jr., President and Chief Executive Officer; Gilbert M. Grosvenor, Chairman of the Board; Nina D. Hoffman, Executive Vice President and President, Books and School Publishing.

PREPARED BY NATIONAL GEOGRAPHIC SCHOOL PUBLISHING
Ericka Markman, Senior Vice President; Steve Mico, Vice President, Editorial Director; Marianne Hiland, Editorial Manager; Jim Hiscott, Design Manager; Kristin Hanneman, Illustrations Manager; Matt Wascavage, Manager of Publishing Services; Sean Philpotts, Production Coordinator.

Production: Clifton M. Brown III, Manufacturing and Quality Control.

PROGRAM DEVELOPMENT—Gare Thompson Associates, Inc.

BOOK DEVELOPMENT—Thomas Nieman, Inc.

CONSULTANTS/REVIEWERS—Dr. Margit E. McGuire, School of Education, Seattle University, Seattle, Washington

BOOK DESIGN—Steven Curtis Design, Inc.

2003 © National Geographic Society

Published by the National Geographic Society
1145 17th Street, N.W.
Washington, D.C. 20036–4688
ISBN: 0-7922-8624-3
Second Printing April, 2004
Printed in Canada

Table of Contents

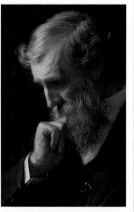

Theodore Roosevelt   *Jane Addams*   *Booker T. Washington*   *John Muir*

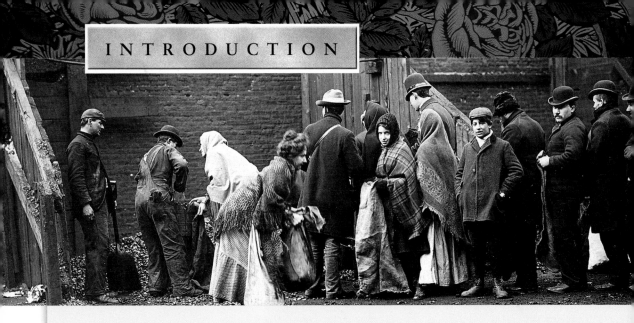

America in 1900

A CHALLENGING TIME

A new century was beginning. Many people felt excited and hopeful about the future. So many things were changing! Wonderful new inventions kept coming. There was the electric light, the telephone, the phonograph, and movies. American business and industry were booming. America's growing cities were exciting places. There was a lot to see and do.

America also had serious problems. Only a small number of people owned most of America's businesses and industries. These owners were becoming very rich. But most workers stayed poor. In addition, many American workplaces were very dangerous places to make a living.

Between 1900 and 1914, millions of **immigrants** came to America. Many of the newcomers were from southern and eastern Europe. Most were unskilled. They took jobs at the lowest levels in factories, mines, and mills. But most of these jobs paid very little. The crowded city neighborhoods of these newcomers often became **slums**.

The Civil War had ended slavery 35 years earlier. But most African Americans were still struggling against poverty and injustice.

America's rapid growth was taking a toll on its **natural resources** too. Forests were being cut down for timber. Lakes and rivers were being polluted by industry.

Because of these and other problems, not everyone felt good about America's future. Some Americans grew angry at the human suffering and waste they saw around them. They wanted to make things better. Their efforts became known as the **Progressive Movement**. These **reformers** all believed that American society needed changing. But they often didn't agree about what those changes should be.

RICH AND POOR

Imagine that you could travel back in time to one of America's big cities in 1900. What do you see? You are surprised to discover that it's not so big. There are tall buildings, but very few over 20 stories high. But it's busy and dirty!

The streets are full of every kind of horse-drawn buggy and delivery wagon. Most people get around in trolley cars. You see only a few automobiles. At night, the streets are still lit mostly by gas lamps. You notice that rich and poor people live very differently.

A RICH NEW YORK CITY NEIGHBORHOOD

Rich families live in large, beautiful houses on wide streets. They have running water, bathtubs, and indoor toilets. Many homes have the new electric lights and telephones.

In poor neighborhoods, the streets are narrow, crowded, and dirty. Families live jammed together in **tenements**, five to seven stories high.

A single house might hold dozens of families. A family of six might live in a single dark, stuffy room. Sometimes they even share it with an extra person or two to help pay the rent. Many families use the same outdoor toilet.

Life seems harder for most people in 1900 than it is today. You are glad to return to the present.

A POOR NEW YORK CITY NEIGHBORHOOD

"Isn't it a fine thing to be alive when so many great things are happening."

Theodore Roosevelt

SHIP OF STATE

A 1902 CARTOON OF ROOSEVELT AS AMERICA'S PILOT

CHAPTER 1

Reformer in the White House

THEODORE ROOSEVELT

ROOSEVELT AS A BOXER IN COLLEGE

O*ne man became a symbol for the Progressive Era.* His name was Theodore Roosevelt. He was president of the United States from 1901 to 1909. He used his office to make things better.

Roosevelt began his life as a weak and sickly child. But when he was 11, his father built a gym for him. Young Teddy spent long hours lifting weights and pounding a punching bag. He also spent a lot of time outdoors and grew to love nature. Teddy became strong and tough. His father also taught him to be concerned for the less fortunate. As a young man, Teddy was eager to try new things. He ran from one activity to another. Teddy's words poured out in a loud, high-pitched voice. He wore thick glasses and had a toothy grin and curly red hair. Teddy made a strong impression wherever he went.

Roosevelt grew up to have all the qualities Americans admired. He was brave and full of energy. He was fair and direct. He was upbeat and believed that with effort and a firm purpose he could fix any problem.

Roosevelt became the leader of the Progressive Movement by being a hands-on president. He was a man of action. People described Roosevelt as "a steam engine in trousers," "a buzz saw," "a cyclone," "an earthquake." He believed that a president should use the power of his office to make changes. Roosevelt worked to make the United States a world power. He forced big business to obey the law. He preserved parts of the great American wilderness. All Americans deserved a **"square deal,"** Roosevelt declared, and he was going to make sure that they got it.

A SQUARE DEAL

Before Roosevelt, American government had made few laws about how businesses should be run. But he changed that. Roosevelt worked to limit the power of big business and make things better for workers.

At this time, American workers usually labored six or even seven days a week, ten hours a day. Pay was low. If business was poor, wages were cut or workers were fired. Workplaces were often dangerous, with few safety rules. Some workers got sick or even died from unhealthy conditions. Injuries were common.

ROOSEVELT ATTACKS BIG BUSINESS.

NO MOLLY-CODDLING HERE

Some workers tried to make things better. They joined together to fight for better working conditions. The groups they formed were called **unions**. The main way they could change things was by walking off the job, or going on **strike**. Some strikes were short and peaceful. But others were long, bitter, and sometimes even violent.

THE COAL STRIKE

Nearly 150,000 miners walked off the job in the coalfields of Pennsylvania in May 1902. They wanted higher pay and an eight-hour work day. But even more, they wanted the mine owners to accept their union. This strike concerned everyone in America. Coal was the fuel that most people used for heat. As winter approached, people became alarmed. Finally, Roosevelt stepped in.

The President asked both sides to end the strike. The workers agreed to discuss the issues. But the owners demanded that Roosevelt send in troops to stop the strike.

Roosevelt answered by saying that he would send in troops. But they would not break the strike. They would take over the mines.

At this threat, the owners backed down. The coal strike was over. The country cheered their president. He had forced the powerful mine owners to do as he wished. But he had done so fairly. In the end, the miners won a nine-hour day and a 10 percent increase in pay.

This was the first time the federal government had played an important role in a strike. Roosevelt had worked to protect the interests of the workers and of the public.

ROOSEVELT AND WORKERS

"The life of men and women is so cheap and property is so sacred. There are so many of us for one job, it matters little if 146 of us are burned to death. It is up to the working people to save themselves."

Rose Schneiderman

TRIANGLE SHIRTWAIST FIRE IN NEW YORK

CHAPTER 2

Reformers in the Workplace

**WOMEN STRIKERS
MARCHING IN A PARADE**

THE SWEATSHOPS

Theodore Roosevelt was a member of the upper class. So were many of the other Progressive Era reformers. But some of the reformers were workers themselves. Among these were women like Polish immigrant Rose Schneiderman. Schneiderman helped organize the female workers in New York City's clothing industry.

The clothing industry was based on small, crowded workplaces called **sweatshops**. Most of the sweatshop workers were women and girls. They worked long hours under poor conditions for low wages. In 1909, women organized a huge strike against the sweatshop owners. The strike brought some gains, but working conditions remained bad. It took a tragedy to show how bad.

Near closing time on March 25, 1911, a fire broke out on the eighth floor of the Triangle Shirtwaist Company. Within minutes, flames raced through the rag-filled aisles of the factory. Workers were trapped. The owners kept most doors locked because they feared workers might leave early or steal.

In less than 15 minutes, 146 workers were dead. Most of them were young women. Many jumped out of the high windows to escape the flames. As a result of this tragedy, officials began to look into working conditions. Laws were passed that improved safety in the workplace and cut down working hours for women and children.

THE NEWSIES

Child workers learned to band together to win fair treatment too. In 1899, boys and girls sold newspapers on every city street corner. These "newsies" yelled out the day's headlines to get people to buy their papers. Most of the children worked after school. But some spent the whole day selling newspapers.

GIRL AND BOY SELLING NEWSPAPERS

William Randolph Hearst and Joseph Pulitzer each owned a major newspaper in New York City. They depended on the newsies to get their papers into the hands of the public. The children bought the papers from the newspaper companies. Then they sold them for just a little more. They kept about a nickel for every ten newspapers they sold. If they had papers left over at the end of the day, they couldn't return them and get their money back.

Then newspaper sales slowed. To make up the difference, Hearst and Pulitzer decided to charge the newsies more for the newspapers.

In July 1899, 300 newsies formed a union. They refused to deliver the newspapers until the price per paper was what it had been.

The strike lasted two weeks. The public supported the children. The newsies became heroes. The strike spread to other states. The owners began to lose a lot of money. Finally, Hearst and Pulitzer gave up. They kept newspaper prices the same as before. The newsies could also return unsold papers. The children had won.

The New York Times.

NEWSBOY WITH DELIVERY BAG

ALGER SERIES No.23
A NEW YORK BOY
by HORATIO ALGER, JR.

DIME NOVEL ABOUT NEWSIES

THE MEATPACKING INDUSTRY

Some of the most dangerous American workplaces were in the meatpacking industry. Upton Sinclair was a writer. In 1904, a magazine sent him to Chicago to study the meatpacking industry there.

Sinclair's goal was to expose bad working conditions. Most of the workers in Chicago were immigrants from eastern Europe. Their work in the meatpacking plants was often very dangerous. Many workers were injured on the job. Others became sick. Sometimes they were overworked. At other times there would be no work at all.

Sinclair put what he learned about the meatpacking industry into a story he called *The Jungle*. It became a best-seller. But what interested—and horrified—the American public was not how the workers suffered. Instead, it was Sinclair's picture of how dirty the meatpacking plants were.

Theodore Roosevelt was as horrified as the rest of the American public. He ordered an investigation of the meatpacking industry. New laws were passed to protect the food Americans ate.

UPTON SINCLAIR

IMMIGRANT WORKERS
STUFFING SAUSAGES
IN A CHICAGO
MEATPACKING PLANT

IN THEIR OWN WORDS

"I aimed at the
public's heart, and
by accident I hit it
in the stomach."

Upton Sinclair

"Our very first Christmas at Hull House, when we as yet knew nothing of child labor, a number of little girls refused the candy which was offered them as part of the Christmas good cheer, saying simply that they worked in a candy factory and could not bear the sight of it."

Jane Addams

Improving the Cities

JANE ADDAMS

*P*oor immigrants were flooding America's big cities around 1900. At this time, the government did very little to help the poor. **Settlement houses** helped fill this need. These were community centers that aided poor people in cities. They fed them, gave health care, ran nursery schools, taught English, and provided many other important services.

HULL HOUSE TODAY

The settlement house movement in America was spread by Jane Addams. She was the daughter of a banker and grew up in comfort.

Addams was well educated. She wanted to use her education to do useful work. But women were expected to stay at home as wives and mothers.

Addams felt she had nothing worthwhile to do. Then she took a tour of Europe. In London, Addams visited settlement houses and found what she was looking for. Here was a way she could help the poor and also help herself. Addams went to Chicago, Illinois. With a friend, she bought an old house in a rundown part of the city. With a lot of hard work, they turned it into Hull House.

HULL HOUSE

Addams brought together many young women who also wanted to do useful work. Within two years, more than 2,000 people were visiting Hull House every week. Because of this success, others tried to do what Addams had done. By 1891, there were six settlement houses in the United States. By 1910, there were over 400.

Addams saw the problems of her poor, crowded neighborhood daily. The streets were filled with garbage. City collectors rarely came around. The mayor appointed Addams as a garbage inspector. She was able to make a number of improvements.

Over time, Addams and Hull House became famous. Many well-known people visited Hull House through the years. One of them was Theodore Roosevelt. Addams helped Roosevelt run for president in 1912. She said he was one of the few men in public life who supported the movement for social justice. Some newspapers said Addams brought Roosevelt a million votes!

ADDAMS SUPPORTING ROOSEVELT FOR PRESIDENT

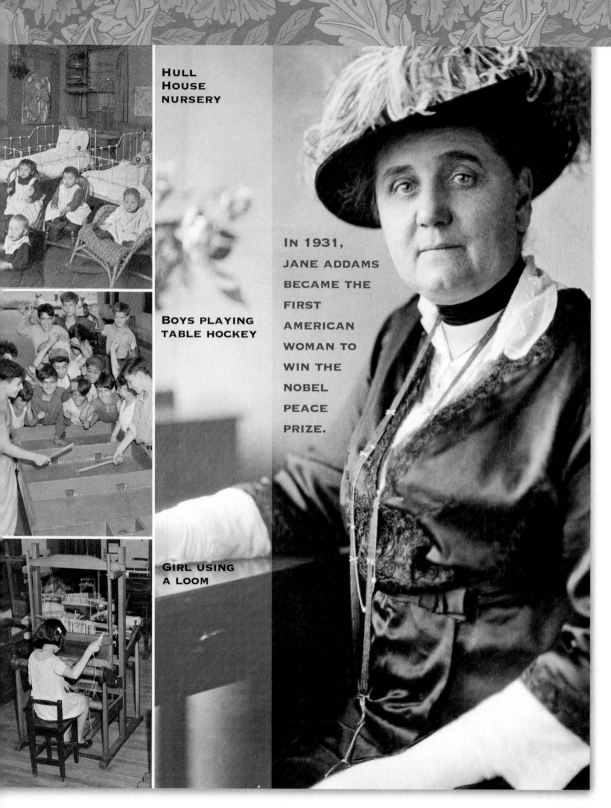

HULL
HOUSE
NURSERY

BOYS PLAYING
TABLE HOCKEY

IN 1931,
JANE ADDAMS
BECAME THE
FIRST
AMERICAN
WOMAN TO
WIN THE
NOBEL
PEACE
PRIZE.

GIRL USING
A LOOM

JACOB RIIS

Like Jane Addams, Jacob Riis (rees) worked to improve the lives of the poor immigrants who lived in city tenements. He did it by picturing poverty in photographs and words. His account shocked Americans.

Riis was born in Denmark in 1849, the son of middle-class parents. He arrived in New York City in 1870. Times were hard when Riis arrived. He was often jobless, homeless, and hungry. Riis finally found work as a police reporter. He covered crime and life in the slums. What he saw made him both sad and angry. He decided to try to make things better for the poor.

In 1887, Riis began to take photographs of people and places on his beat. Several years later, he wrote *How the Other Half Lives*. The "Other Half" are the poor. Riis used photographs and descriptions to paint a powerful picture. His book helped convince lawmakers to force slum landlords to clean up their buildings. One of the most famous people inspired by Riis's book was Theodore Roosevelt. He worked with Riis to improve conditions in New York City.

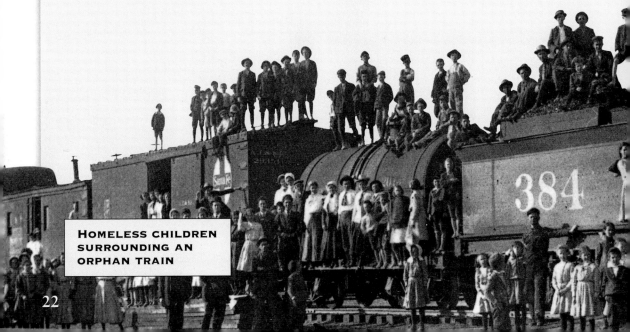

HOMELESS CHILDREN SURROUNDING AN ORPHAN TRAIN

THE ORPHAN TRAINS

Jacob Riis photographed many homeless children. He found some of them living on the streets. He found others living in lodging houses run by the Children's Aid Society. Riis admired the work of the Society.

In 1854, the Society's director had started a program to help homeless children. It was called "placing out." Trains would carry the children west. At towns along the way, farm families could choose a child to bring home. In return, the child would help with the daily chores.

Riis wrote glowing descriptions of poor children finding warm and welcoming new families. And most did find good homes. Between 1854 and 1929, more than 100,000 children rode the "orphan trains."

Homes For Children
WANTED

A Company of Homeless Children from the East Will Arrive at

McPherson, Friday, September 15.

These children are of various ages and of both sexes, having been thrown friendless upon the world. They come under the auspices of the Children's Aid Society, of New York. They are well disciplined, having come from various orphanages. The citizens of this community are asked to assist the agent in finding good homes for them. Persons taking these children must be recommended by the local committee. They must treat the children in every way as members of the family, sending them to school, church, Sabbath school and properly clothe them until they are 18 years old. Protestant children placed in Protestant homes and Catholic children in Catholic homes. The following well known citizens have agreed to act as a local committee to aid the agents in securing homes:

Dr. Heaston
F. A. Vaniman

H. A. Rowland
W. J. Krehbiel

C. W. Bachelor
K. Sorensen

Applications must be made to and endorsed by the local committee.

An address will be given by the agents. Come and see the children and hear the address. Distribution will take place at

Opera House, Friday, September 15

NOTICE OF ARRIVING ORPHAN TRAIN

Photographs

In his photographs, Riis showed the world of New York City's poor to a shocked America.

LAUNDRY HANGING BEHIND A TENEMENT

JACOB RIIS

PEDDLER'S "BEDROOM" BEHIND A SLUM BUILDING

ITALIAN IMMIGRANT
MOTHER AND BABY

A POOR NEIGHBORHOOD IN NEW YORK CITY

YOUNG AFRICAN-AMERICAN SHARECROPPERS

Fighting for Equality

UP FROM SLAVERY

The Civil War ended slavery. But it did not end injustice to African Americans. By 1900, life was better for them in a number of ways. More black children were now in school. More African-American families owned their own homes. More African Americans owned small businesses. These included food stores, barbershops, restaurants, and real estate offices.

But many problems still remained. Most African Americans lived in the South. In the late 1800s, Southern whites passed many laws limiting freedom for African Americans. Schools, hotels, trains, streetcars, theaters, and restaurants were **segregated**, or separated by race. Few African Americans could vote or serve on juries.

There were many jobs that were off limits to them too. Even worse, African Americans were always in danger from the racial violence of **lynching**. Southern mobs would hang African Americans for the slightest offenses.

Most African Americans were very poor. They worked as **sharecroppers** on farms and plantations. The work was hard and brought little reward. The sharecroppers were usually in debt to the landowners, who often cheated them.

Booker T. Washington and W. E. B. Du Bois (doo BOYZ) were African-American reformers. They both wanted to solve these problems. But they had very different ideas about how to do it.

BOOKER T. WASHINGTON

Booker T. Washington was born a slave on a small farm in Virginia. Through great efforts, he got an education and became a teacher. In 1881, Washington founded Tuskegee Institute in Alabama as a school for African Americans. Male students learned such skills as farming, carpentry, and blacksmithing. Female students learned cooking and sewing. Many Tuskegee graduates became teachers.

In 1895, Washington made a speech to a largely white audience in Atlanta, Georgia. At the end of his speech, the audience cheered. He had said just what they wanted to hear. African Americans should be patient. They should wait to fight for the vote and other civil rights. They should first learn practical skills that would help them get jobs.

After his Atlanta speech, Washington became the most famous and powerful African American of his day. He tried to use his fame and power to help other African Americans.

CARTOON OF WASHINGTON AND ROOSEVELT AT THE WHITE HOUSE

Washington was invited to speak around the country. Many political leaders admired him. President Theodore Roosevelt asked him to dinner at the White House in 1901. Roosevelt called him "a genius" and consulted with him on racial matters.

These connections helped Washington do some good things. He was able to raise a lot of money for Tuskegee Institute. Washington also worked quietly to fight segregation. He tried to help more African Americans get the vote. He kept these efforts quiet for fear that white people would no longer help him.

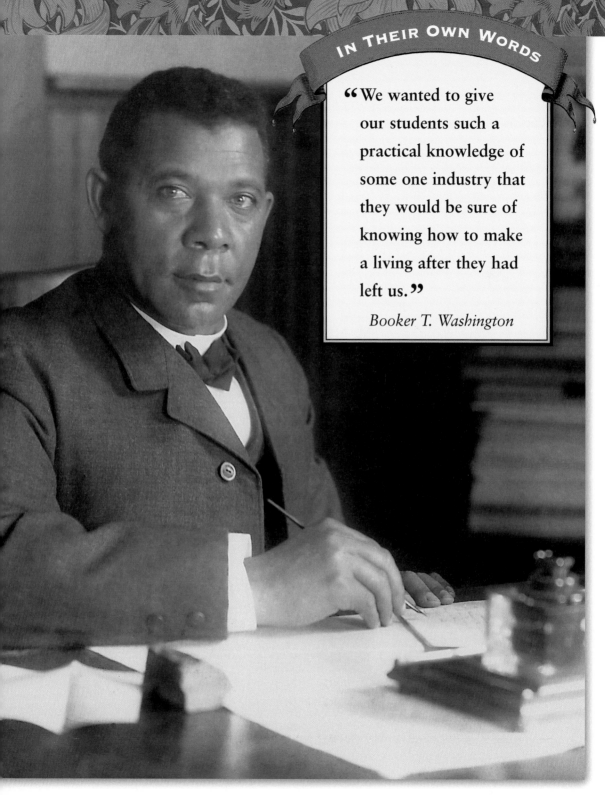

"We wanted to give our students such a practical knowledge of some one industry that they would be sure of knowing how to make a living after they had left us."

Booker T. Washington

W.E.B. DU BOIS

W. E. B. Du Bois had a very different background from Washington. Du Bois was born in 1868 in Massachusetts. Few black families lived in his town. His friends were mostly white.

After high school, Du Bois won a scholarship to Fisk University in Nashville, Tennessee. For the first time, Du Bois saw Southern racism. He wanted to end this injustice. After graduation from Fisk, he went on to study at Harvard University. He then became a professor at Atlanta University in Georgia.

Du Bois wrote many articles expressing his ideas. He believed that African Americans needed to use politics to win their rights. He also talked about the "talented tenth." These were the brightest and most able African Americans. The "talented tenth" must go to college. They would be the leaders to help other African Americans.

DU BOIS IN HIS OFFICE

In 1909, Du Bois and other Progressive leaders founded the National Association for the Advancement of Colored People (NAACP). One of these leaders was Jane Addams. The NAACP's goal was to win equal rights, including the right to vote, for all African Americans. The NAACP also fought racial violence, such as lynching.

Du Bois gave up teaching to work for the NAACP. He became the editor of *The Crisis*, the NAACP's magazine. He published political articles along with poetry and stories by African-American writers. *The Crisis* became very successful. It made Du Bois famous. He replaced Booker T. Washington as the most important African-American leader.

"I believe in liberty for all men; the space to stretch their arms and their soul; the right to breathe and the right to vote; the freedom to choose their friends, enjoy the sunshine, and ride on the railroads, uncursed by color."

W. E. B. Du Bois

How Should African Americans Win Equality?

Booker T. Washington and W. E. B. Du Bois came to stand for opposite points of view on how African Americans should win equal rights.

Washington believed that African Americans should focus on learning trades and making money. He thought their growing economic power would help them win equal rights at some point in the future. He felt African Americans should put up with segregation in the meantime.

Our greatest danger is that, in the great leap from slavery to freedom, we may overlook the fact that the masses of us are to live by the productions of our hands.

No race can prosper till it learns that there is as much dignity in tilling a field as in writing a poem. It is at the bottom of life we must begin, and not at the top.

SEWING CLASS AT TUSKEGEE

Du Bois felt that Washington's plan suggested that African Americans were fit only to work with their hands, and not with their minds. He did not agree that going along with segregation would win equality for African Americans. He believed that they must demand their rights immediately in order to keep their self-respect.

I would not deny the necessity of teaching the Negro to work. Nevertheless, the object of all true education is not to make men carpenters, it is to make carpenters men. Education must not simply teach work—it must teach Life.

The way for a people to gain their reasonable rights is not by voluntarily throwing them away.

NAACP MARCH AGAINST LYNCHING

History has generally favored Du Bois's point of view. He was an important influence on the African-American civil rights movement of the 1950s and 1960s.

"No temple made with hands can compare with Yosemite. Every rock in its walls seems to glow with life."

John Muir

YOSEMITE VALLEY IN CALIFORNIA

CHAPTER 5

Saving the Land

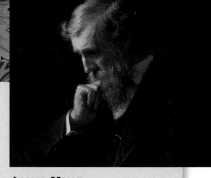

JOHN MUIR

The Progressives were not only interested in improving cities and workplaces. They also wanted to change the way America's natural resources were being used—and abused.

Few people thought that the nation's resources would ever run out. By the late 1800s, some people's thinking began to change. More than half of America's forests had been cut down. Factories were pouring out smoke and dumping waste. Miners were stripping away large areas to get to the minerals underground. So much was being destroyed that people began to worry. A movement started up to preserve what was left of the wilderness. It was called the **conservation movement**. One man became its leader. His name was John Muir (myoor).

Muir loved the wilderness. He spent years wandering alone thousands of miles on foot through the untouched mountains and forests of the West. In 1868, Muir first visited Yosemite (yoh–SEHM–uh–tee) Valley in California's Sierra Nevada mountain range. It became his favorite place.

Muir worked to save the American wilderness. He wrote articles and made speeches. In 1890, he helped establish Yosemite as a national park. Two years later, Muir became president of the newly formed Sierra Club. Its goal was to preserve the wilderness.

JOHN MUIR

ROOSEVELT AND MUIR

When Theodore Roosevelt became president, Muir found he had gained an important friend. Roosevelt was the first president to pay attention to America's natural resources. He loved the outdoors. He was a hiker, a camper, and a hunter. He wanted to save the nation's natural resources.

So, in the spring of 1903, Roosevelt asked Muir to guide him through Yosemite. The two camped out and rode horses through the mountains. When they awoke after a second night of camping, they were covered with four inches of snow. Roosevelt called it "the grandest day of my life!" And the two men never stopped talking.

Roosevelt returned to Washington full of Muir's ideas. He followed up by using the power of the government to set aside 5 national parks, 18 national monuments, and 148 million acres of national forest.

A MAGAZINE COVER SHOWING TOURISTS AT THE GRAND CANYON IN 1911

"The American had but one thought about a tree, and that was to cut it down."

Theodore Roosevelt

PRESIDENT ROOSEVELT WITH JOHN MUIR IN YOSEMITE NATIONAL PARK

BALANCING INTERESTS

Roosevelt and Muir did not agree about everything. Roosevelt wanted to save the wilderness; but he also believed in its "wise use." Gifford Pinchot was the chief of the Forest Service under Roosevelt. He shared Roosevelt's practical approach. Pinchot believed that federal land should serve "the greatest number." He wanted to open certain federal lands to lumbering, mining, and grazing. As Pinchot put it, "Wilderness is waste."

Muir and Pinchot found themselves on opposite sides of an important fight. The city of San Francisco wanted to build a reservoir to store water by flooding a beautiful valley. Pinchot wanted the reservoir. Muir fought to save the valley. In the end, Muir lost. He died not long afterward at the age of 76. But Muir helped the American people see the value of the wilderness. As he expressed it, "In God's wildness lies the hope of the world."

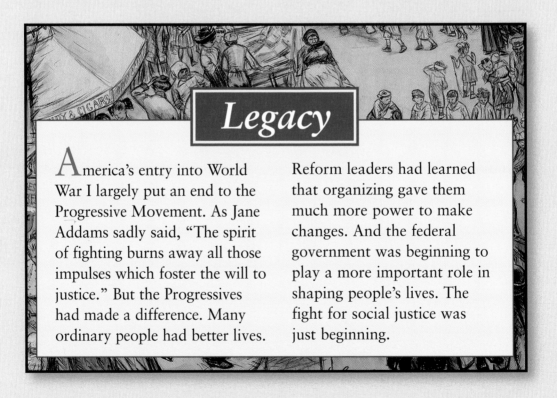

Legacy

America's entry into World War I largely put an end to the Progressive Movement. As Jane Addams sadly said, "The spirit of fighting burns away all those impulses which foster the will to justice." But the Progressives had made a difference. Many ordinary people had better lives.

Reform leaders had learned that organizing gave them much more power to make changes. And the federal government was beginning to play a more important role in shaping people's lives. The fight for social justice was just beginning.

Glossary

CONSERVATION MOVEMENT a movement to preserve and manage natural resources

IMMIGRANT a person who settles in a new country

LYNCHING putting a person to death, usually by hanging, without a lawful trial

NATURAL RESOURCE something found in nature that is a source of wealth to a country

PROGRESSIVE MOVEMENT a reform movement beginning in the late 1800s that tried to correct many economic and social problems in American life

REFORMER a person who tries to improve society

SEGREGATE separate, often by race

SETTLEMENT HOUSE a community center helping people, often immigrants, in poor neighborhoods

SHARECROPPER a tenant farmer who works the land for a share of the crop

SLUM an overcrowded, run-down part of a city

"SQUARE DEAL" Theodore Roosevelt's program of reform as president

STRIKE an organized act of stopping work to force employers to grant workers' demands

SWEATSHOP a small, crowded workplace where employees work long hours under poor conditions for low wages

TENEMENT a building in a poor section of a city that is divided into sets of rooms in which different families live

UNION a group of workers united to win higher pay and better working conditions

Index